Harmonious Modes

Printed in the United States of America

First Printing, 2014

ISBN-10 1503367746
ISBN-13 978-1503367746

Webdinger Press
Bozeman, MT 59715

www.webdinger.com

Harmonious Modes

by Kelly Mullins

Table of Contents

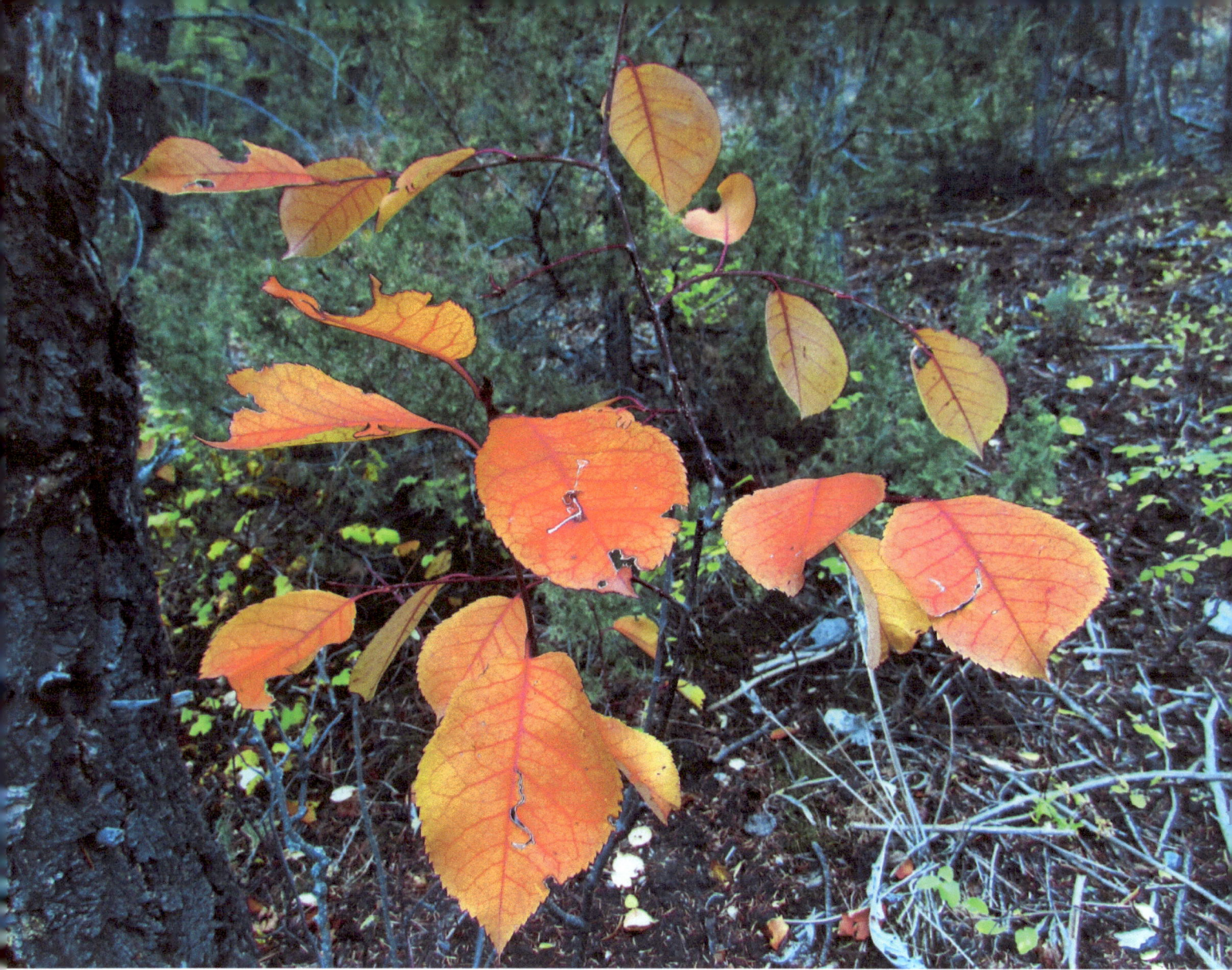

"Better than a thousand
hollow words,
is
one word
that brings
peace."

- Buddha

Clarity. It was what he needed. His life had become out of control and as a result, he could not find his glasses. He had no clue where they might be or when he last wore them. But that was how it was going for him lately. Without his glasses, everything had fuzzy edges. Even when he squinted and forced the muscles in his eyeballs to contract, nothing was clear.

It was a perfect metaphor.

A month ago, James was a rock star. His guitar was more than just an instrument. He felt it in his nerves. It became aroused when his fingers slid up and down the neck pressing frets with blind precision. He became aroused when it responded with the pristine, sweet sounds he knew it would produce. He did not just play his guitar; he made love to it; he blended with it and they became one.

But he lost that too. Actually, it was stolen from the tour van… along with half the other equipment. When they realized they had been victims of theft in a dirty alley behind some grungy venue in Omaha, Nebraska, the band started to fall apart on the spot. Looking back, James realized that the whole tour had taken its toll on them. Omaha was nothing more than the last straw.

Calling the cops was out of the question. They had all drank a bit too much. Smoked some good weed. Creeper. Some scrawny little hottie had hooked him up with a couple lines and let him fondle her tits while he signed them with a sharpie. Danny found some dude with skag and took off for the night.

Odd to think that that was when life seemed so clear. After the partying was done, the show was over and it was time load equipment, it all changed. The passenger window of the van was shattered and the side door left open. Ben blamed Danny for taking off. Sheridan blamed Ben for waiting so goddammed long to pack up his drums. James did not care who was to blame or how it could have been prevented. Truth was, blame belonged to all of them. He only knew his guitar was gone.

It was in the middle of the escalating shouting match between Sheridan and Ben that he felt rage begin to boil. He wanted to hit something, someone… but he wouldn't do that. He knew that outwardly, he most likely looked bored, but his blood was on fire and his lungs compressed and stiff. Neither Ben nor Sheridan noticed him walk away. That was a month ago.

He walked all night long, west in interstate 80.

He walked for five days. He thought he might die the first day. He couldn't be sure, but he thought it was the bad ole DT's. Needless to say, he did not walk that day. He spent it curled up in a ball under a bridge. If there was anything resembling civilization in this godforsaken flat stretch of nothing, he might have even gone to some ER, but there wasn't and he didn't. The second day was awful as well, but   He spent nights under bridges. He had no money, so he only ate what he could steal from some shitty little convenience store somewhere in the time-warp land of Nebraska.

He made it to Denver when he gave up completely. He found himself sitting on a splintery wooden bench in a shady neighborhood near the downtown area when two massive cro-mag skinheads tried to mug him. When they learned he didn't have anything to steal, they stomped him. Beat him bloody.

He just wanted to die. Just let this shit end…

It was time to ask for help. So he called the last person alive who would want to hear from him: his brother Duane. Duane was the good one. He was a year younger than James, but he was a college graduate and a professional with a sweet six-figure income that he spent on his wife and two kids. The dude lived in Montana. The last time they had talked was bad. Real bad. James had made a complete ass of himself at a family reunion hosted by good ole Mr. Prim on his ten acre mountain mansion property. James had drank way too much and didn't have anything hard to offset the belidgering effects booze had on him. So he started picking fights with anyone he could. It was Duane's wife who received the final lash from James's burning tongue, so Mr. Prim set down his façade long enough to provide a quick pummel. It wasn't a decent ass whipping, but it was enough to cause a silence in the crowd as he lay on the ground bleeding from his nose. Duane gave him the choice of leaving freely or be taken by Montanan law enforcement. Duane's last words to James was, "You and I are done."

But Duane was all he had. His last hope.

"Hello?" James felt unexpected relief at hearing his brother's voice. He didn't say anything at first. What could he say? Hey brother! I know I've been a complete dick to you over the years, but let's put that all aside and what say you send me some money so I can squat in a hotel and spend it all on coke?

"Who's this?"

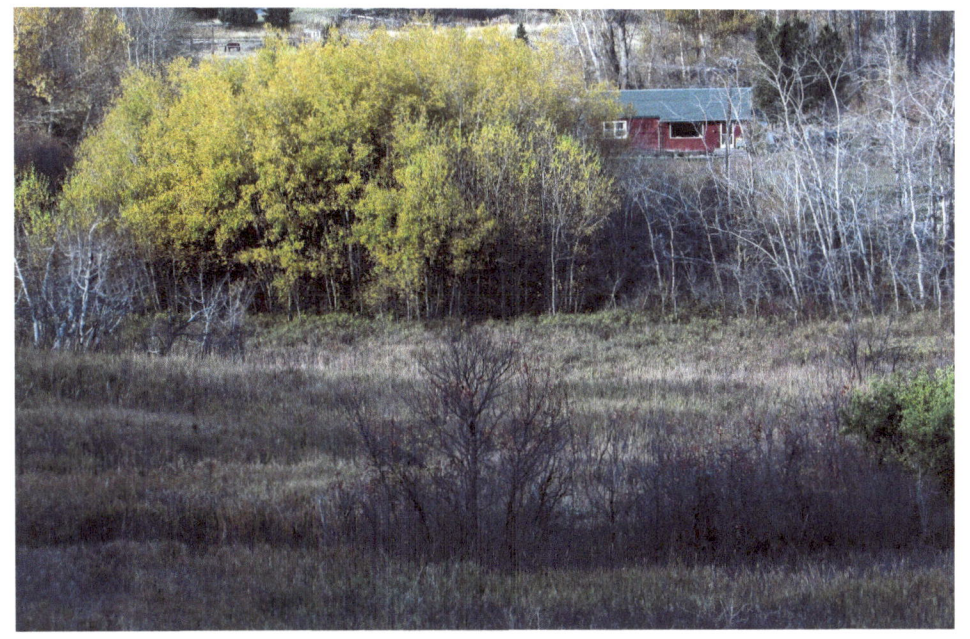

"I… I'm sorry… D… Duane. I'm sorry."

"James? Is that you?"

"Uh, yeah. I'm sorry," he didn't realize he had started sobbing until he was already in the middle of it, "So sorry."

"Whoah… what's goin' on? Where are you?"

"Denver… I'm… in Denver. I just got jumped."

"Calm down, Jimmy. Tell me what happened."

James did his best to tell his brother what had happened and by the end of the conversation, he felt relief. Something he hadn't felt in a very long time. By the end of the conversation, Duane reluctantly agreed to fly James – under the absolute strictest conditions – to Montana.

And that's where he has been for the last three weeks. It had now been a month since he tasted any booze; smoked any weed; snorted, swallowed and lit anything. He felt horrible. Today, he decided – on Duane's very pointed advice – to take up hiking. He found a few trail descriptions online and picked one that was close and seemed fairly easy.

It turned out not to be so easy. Halfway up, he passed out. When he woke, his eyes focused on a flower. The edges of the petals seemed so sharp, the colors so vivid and he was amazed for a moment at the simplicity and beauty of it. Deep from within, something whispered to him. It told him that he was like that flower. That he had sharp, clear edges as well, even though he couldn't necessarily see them. What came next was most surprising to him... gratitude. It was the first thing he had seen clearly since that night a month ago when his life ended. It was a feeling he could not remember ever having felt before. Gratitude. He was grateful to be alive. To be laying on a mountain trail looking at a wild flower.

His life was just beginning.

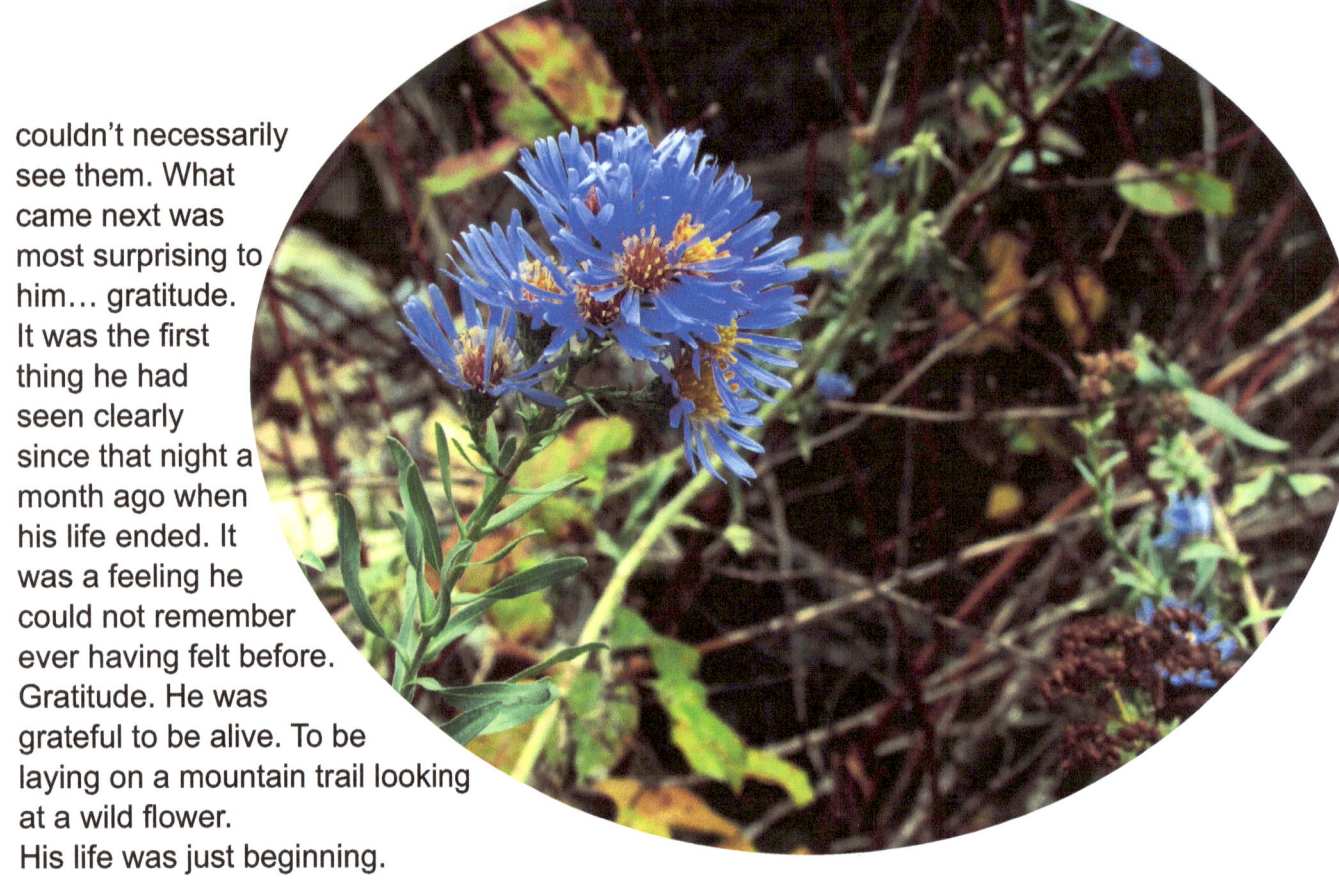

We are not big yet

We are not big yet. But we are growing.
We have not filled in our feet
that want to walk across,
no, stomp across the Universe.
We want to know it all,
and plant our flag in every
orbiting rock in the vast black skies above.
We want to create insight,
yet we are made by it.
Because we are not big yet.
We are little.
We are fragile.
We are small.

I've heard it said the energy released
by a hydrogen bomb is roughly equal to the energy stored in the atoms
Of one kitten: helpless; defenseless,
lost, like us, in blind courage
and entirely unafraid…
maybe not like we should to be.
No, we play. We tear across the comfort of living room carpet
We walk on shaky legs, unfamiliar with gravity
and look out into the Universe with eyes barely opened
where we see so much and want to touch it all,
to feel it with our paws.

I've heard it said one second of our sun is like a billion kittens.
One billion kittens brightly shining at the center
of orbiting bodies of quiet ancient gods
and we yearn to play with them,
to wake them up.
A billion kittens grow gardens and rainforests and
sunburns on treeless beaches when we left the sunscreen in the car, too far away to
bother with.
They do it with a gaze.
One billion kittens hissing,
trapped in layers of atmosphere
bouncing from stratosphere to troposphere
stopping at the tropopause to lick their paws
before growing hot with frustration,
arching backs and batting attacks with needle toes at skin exposed to the unintended
rage
of one billion kittens who define the shade,
while scratching cancers more and more as
days pass deeper into the
frayed, twisting ends of this story.

But their rage is not our fault…
because we are not big yet.
We are only now just learning to walk.
We hobble on shaky legs unaccustomed to gravity.
We open brand new eyes and look out
beyond the blueness of the skies we see
to the center of a galaxy we cannot quite reach.
And there we see a black hole equal to
billions of billions of kittens
stretching limbs quietly feeding on stars
lapping from the Milky Way oblivious to me and you.
To these billions of billions of kittens we are no threat.
And they pose no threat,

though they scratch small rips in the skin of thin membranes separating dimensions
where anything is possible and the least of all that is real is also probable.
They pose no threat though they
crush planets, suns and star systems
absorbing them; dwarfing them;
batting at ticking neutron stars like
little balls with bells.
But they pose us no threat.
They're just doing what billions of
billions of would kittens do.
And we want to play with them,
to rub against their singularity and
claim it as our own.
We want to see the light that cannot
escape
the event of our own horizon
and if we could we would witness
everything between our feet and
the still collective of those billions of
billions of kittens way out there...
If we could truly see we would
witness
just how small we really are.

Maybe one day we'll be as big as them.
We will seek no longer only the comforts of living room carpets.
We'll be grown up cats prancing under the clean air of unblemished ozone.
We will walk confidently in lighted rooms
in palaces made of unity;
built on foundations solid in harmonies of
songs sung by the ancient gods themselves.
We will properly fear our ignorance
but still choose to gently poke at Ursa Major.
We will feel the stars rolling around in the palms of our hands and ask for nothing
in return.

We will be a billion cats safely illuminating lazy summer beaches
and one day, far… far off into the ever expanding future,
we will collide with all that we could wish to be.
We will venture into the great divide between
ignorance and I and we...
... and we will become.

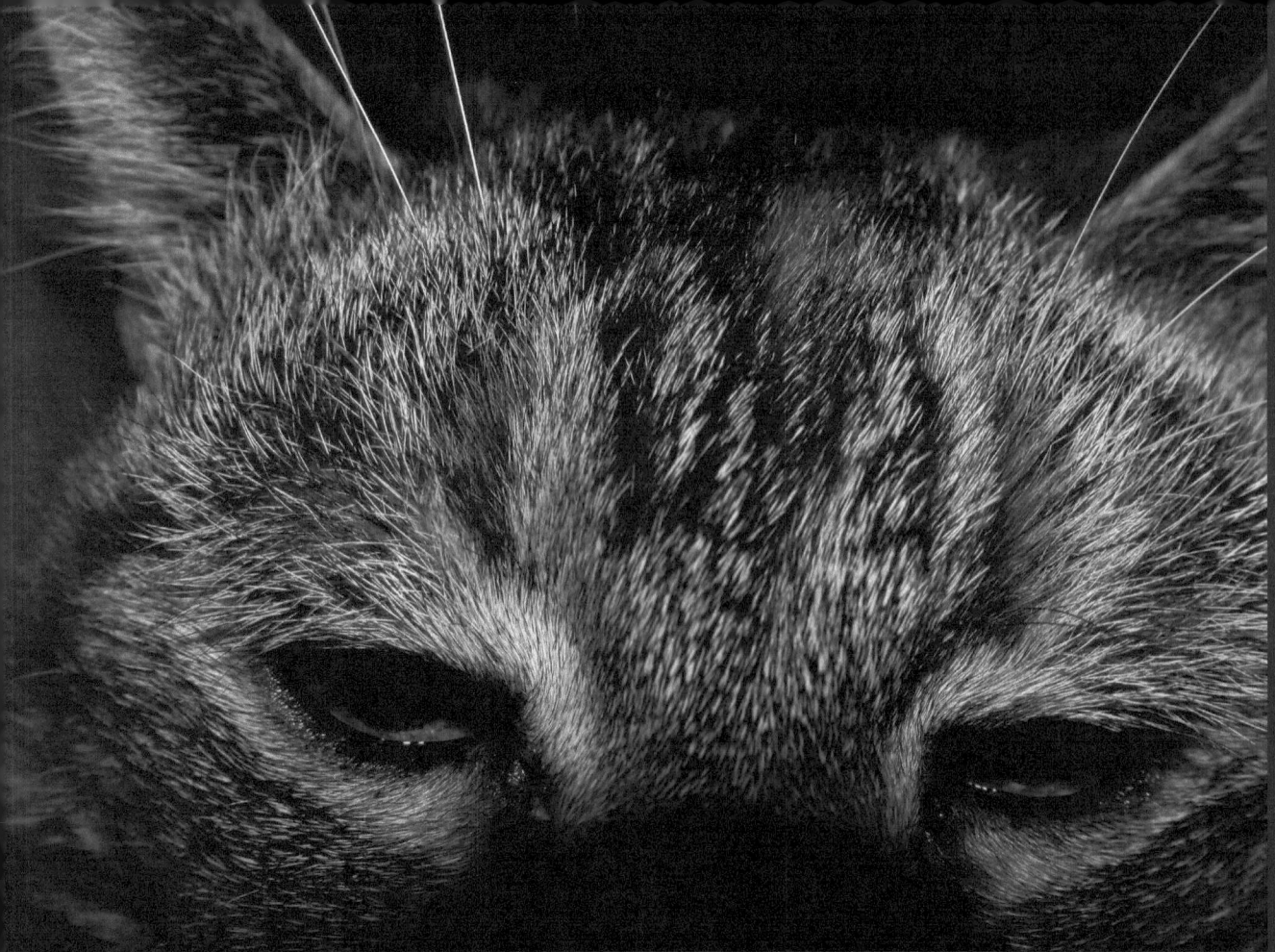

Like billions of billions of kittens we
Won't cry over the sweeping arms
of the Milky Way, spilt way out there.
We won't fret plastic waste and worry
about sore paws that can't do enough
to make things the way they ought to be.
We won't hiss and bat each other on the head
to protect a scrap of petroleum.
We will turn our cheeks, but only for bathing kisses
because we'll be all grown up and in love with everything.
We'll run on sturdy legs, racing gravitational waves to the center of every galaxy.

But for now, we are still too small.
We are only the power of one kitten.
We are weak, but fearless.
Power enough to end a war
to divert one when we're lucky –
power enough to make one –
We have kitten ideals not yet fully developed.
One kitten clutching lives like balls of yarn
With frayed ends twisting to the end of this story,
We are not as big as we feel.
We are not big yet.
But we are growing.

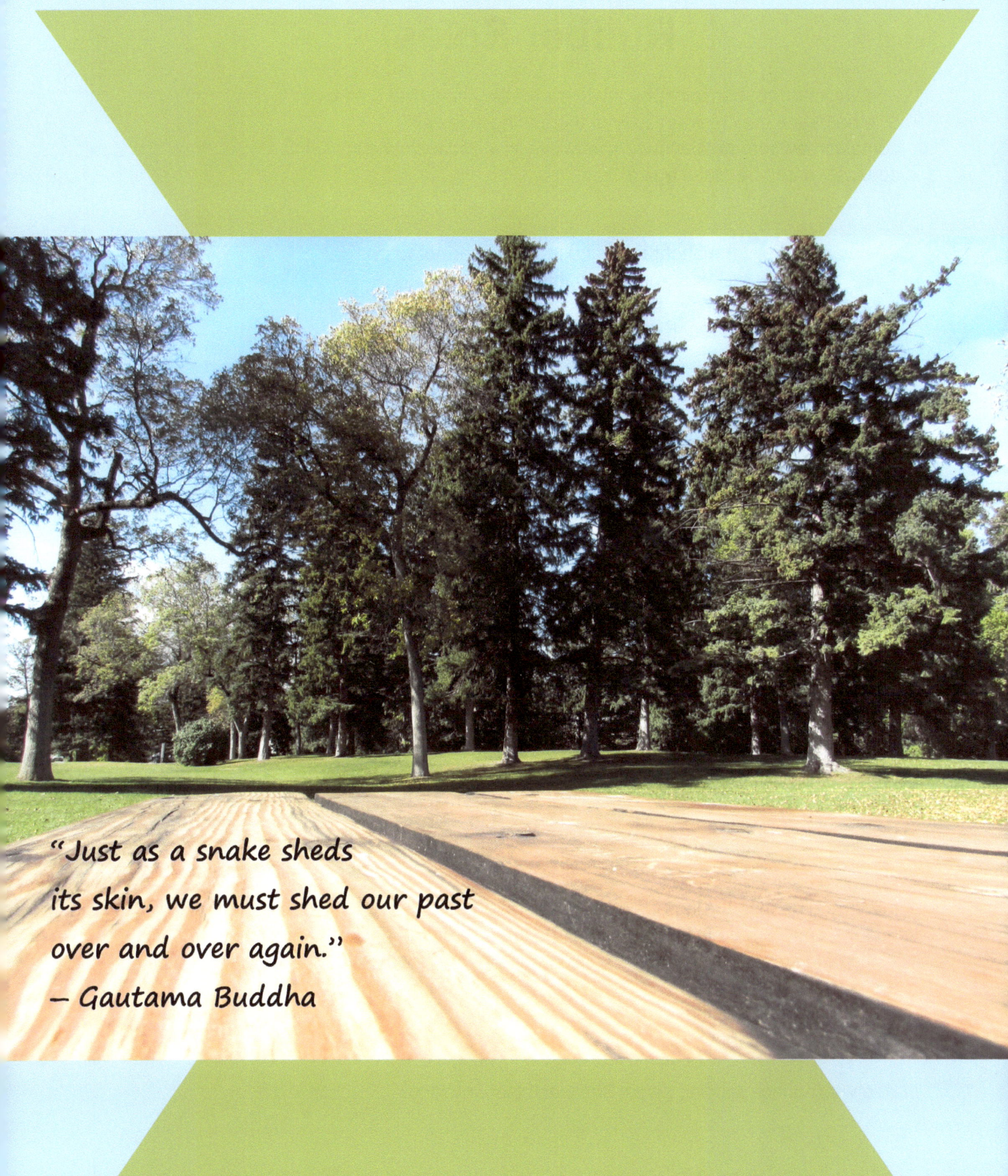

"Just as a snake sheds its skin, we must shed our past over and over again."
— Gautama Buddha

Rubber Soles

She walks on rubber soles, barely there feeding air to her cold toes
She beats the concrete sections of the ruining sidewalk
going somewhere not because she wants to -- because she
doesn't want to be alone again.
She doesn't want to feel.

She waits. Obeys the bright red hand that tells her not to go.
Twice she guesses her purpose with this forced pause
but a third guess changes to a bright white devil over her shoulder
urging her to plow through the cold slush covered asphalt.
She swallows fear.

She doesn't think
about the ground
she feels through
worn socks
worn three days in
a row wet from
sweat and snow.
She doesn't wish
for new shoes nor
the good ol' days
when trips to
friends' were
made in the back
seat of her mom's
car.
She wants not to
be alone.

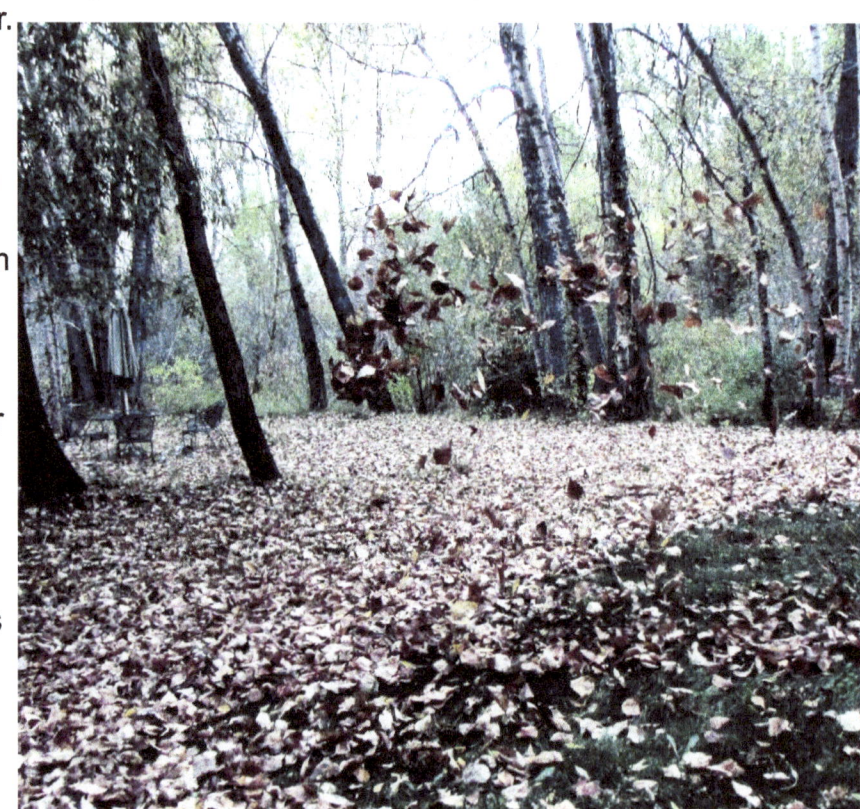

So she crosses
the street, despite having numb feet and broken soles
and the knowledge of the hurt she'll cause by a belly full of
something someone will give her. From something she smoked. Something
drank.
She's thinking about those days in a new school when no one knew her name.
She won't know what it was.

She won't notice slipping away. She won't feel anything.

Doppler

I stood there by the side of the road
smoking with a friend when a car
sped by. Two singing girls bellowed
loudly -- too flat and off key by far.
It seemed probably they had too much
sugar in their coffee is what I suspect
and maybe they had a donut lunch
but thank God for the Doppler effect

because it changed their pitch. I'm not
complaining, because I can't sing at all
and I was happy to see them having fun.
Our conversation paused as I thought
about all those times I tried to wail
out too late with no light of the sun.

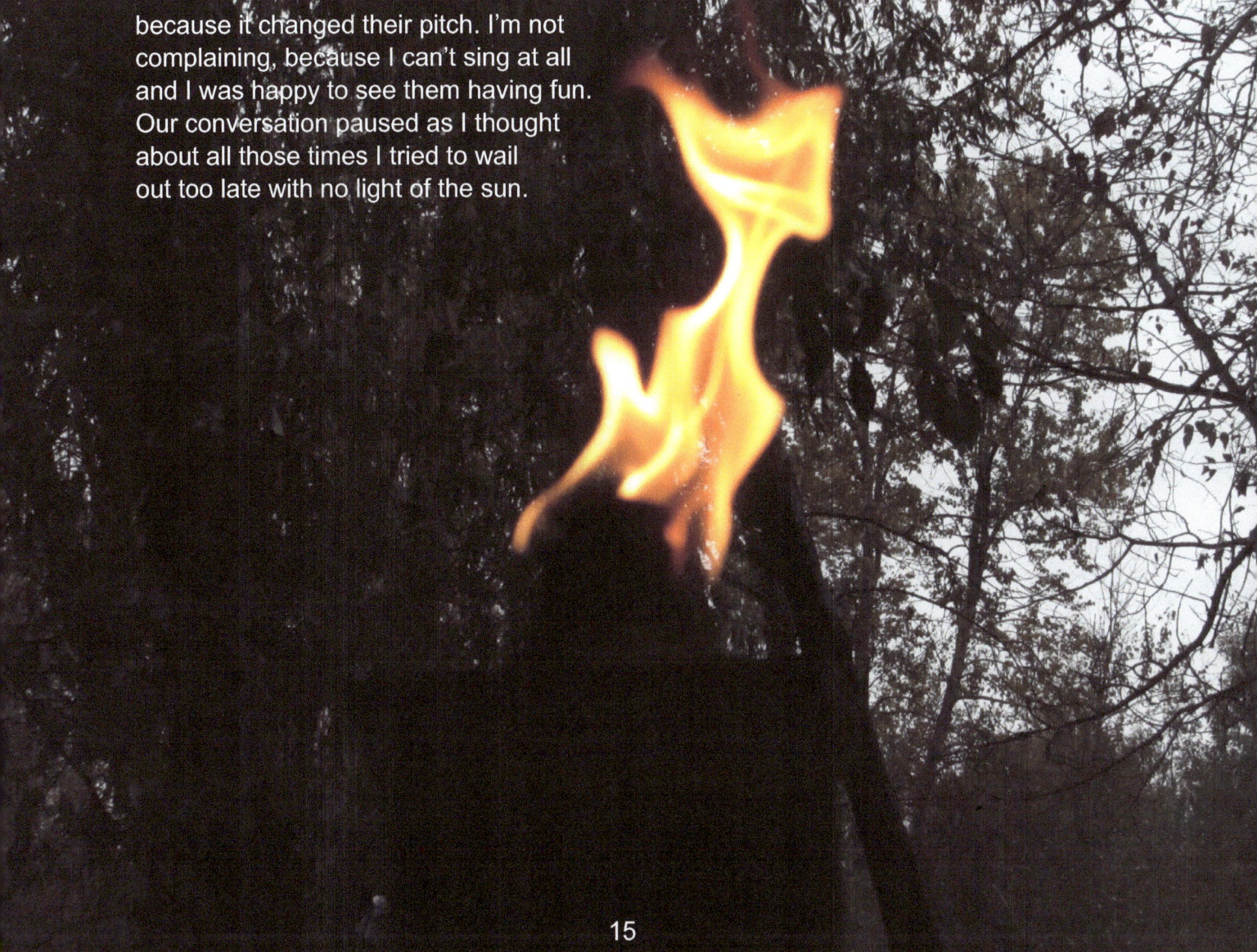

Fashionista

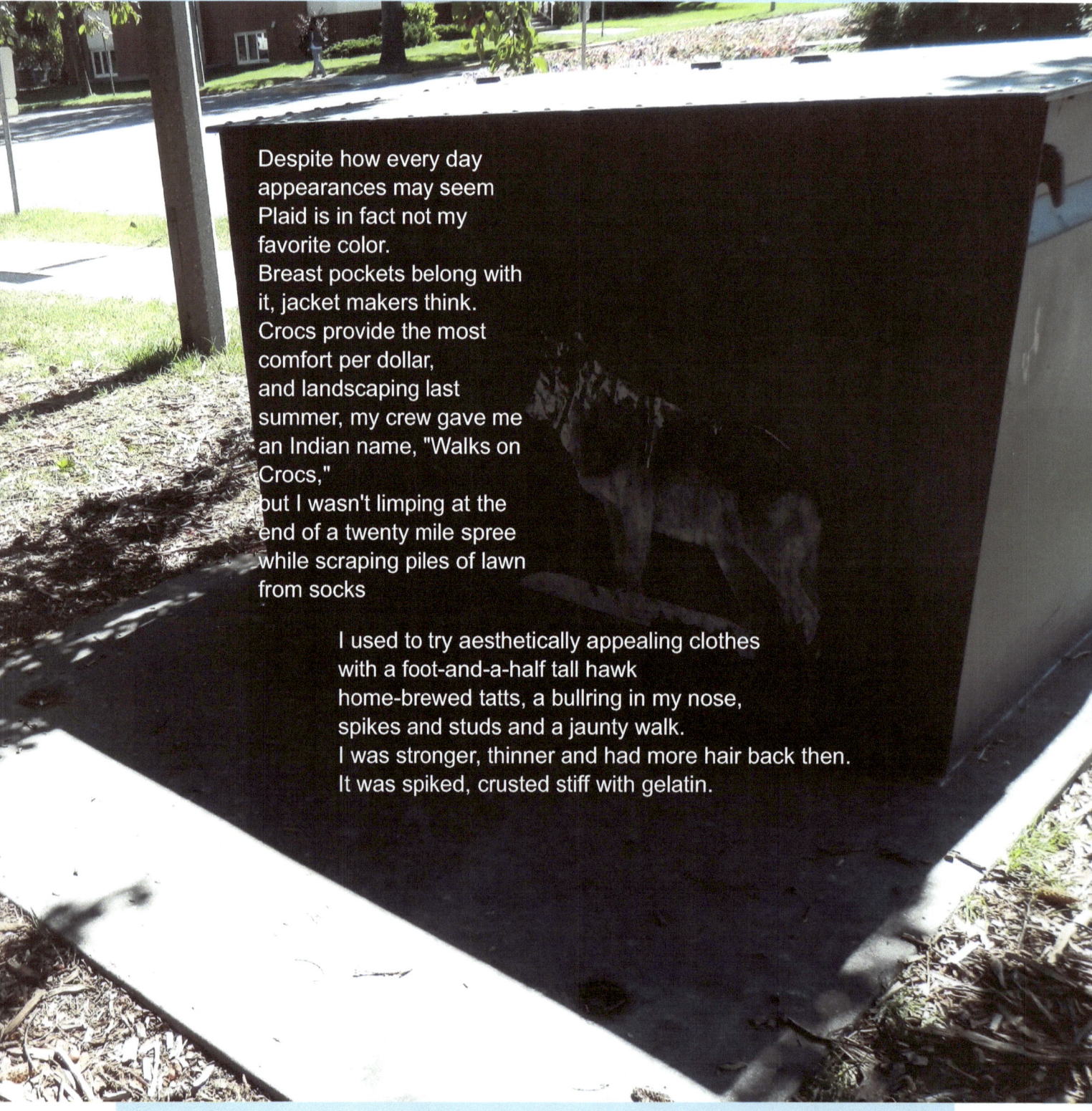

Despite how every day
appearances may seem
Plaid is in fact not my
favorite color.
Breast pockets belong with
it, jacket makers think.
Crocs provide the most
comfort per dollar,
and landscaping last
summer, my crew gave me
an Indian name, "Walks on
Crocs,"
but I wasn't limping at the
end of a twenty mile spree
while scraping piles of lawn
from socks

     I used to try aesthetically appealing clothes
     with a foot-and-a-half tall hawk
     home-brewed tatts, a bullring in my nose,
     spikes and studs and a jaunty walk.
     I was stronger, thinner and had more hair back then.
     It was spiked, crusted stiff with gelatin.

Sole

This is my meditation.
I bought a new pair of shoes –
more than I could afford,
but worth it for the brand: known, trusted
tested on television by celebrity athletes.
Must have value?
They replaced my old pair of shoes which cost
a few bucks on a whim,
and fit my funny fat feet with ease,
but suffered trauma on rocky dirt trails:
their soles had worn down, though still enough
soul to reach a peak.
The old shoes have no holes.

The new shoes – each one – split down the sides,
spilling me into puddles, slipping down dusty trails,
gasping for air. They did not need so much.
This was right around the time they began to fit.
It took too long for me to love them and them me.
They were there because my old shoes are no more.

So, I bought another new pair of shoes on a whim
For just a few bucks.
Same brand as my old shoes.
They are hard and painful.
They are cold an inflexible.
They will not tear, but will not run.
They care nothing for the trail.
Nothing for my feet.
Nothing for me.

In despair, I sat on a bench wishing.
I wanted to be on the trail.
In the midst of my sadness,
I bowed my head to weep and took in the sight of my bare feet.
They looked strong,
ready to run, to skip, to dance beyond the peaks
of my trials and carry me to where
my path lay.
My feet had no tears.
They wanted me as much as I did.

So it doesn't matter what shoes I wear now.
Inside them are the feet willing to carry me
where I need to be despite
how either of us feel.

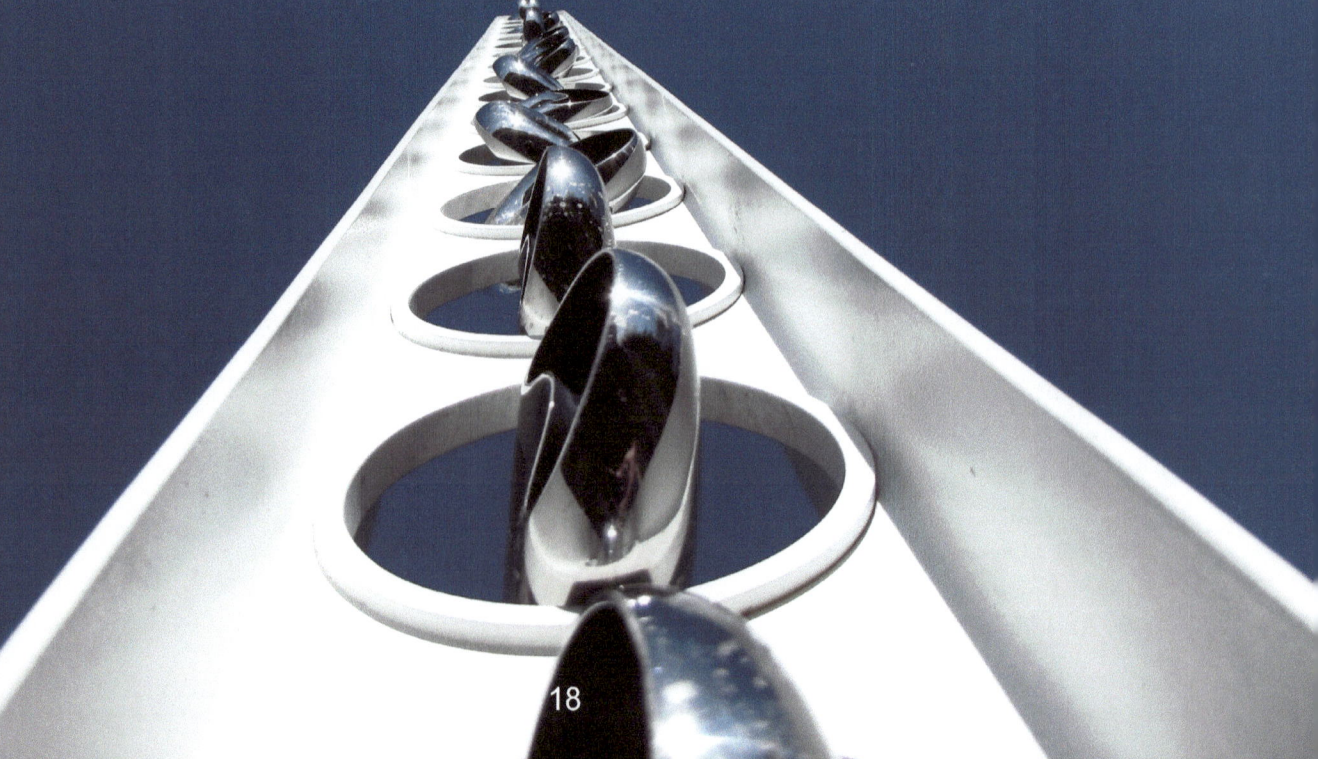

"In the sky, there is no distinction of east and west; people create distinctions out of their own minds and then believe them to be true."

--Guatama Buddha

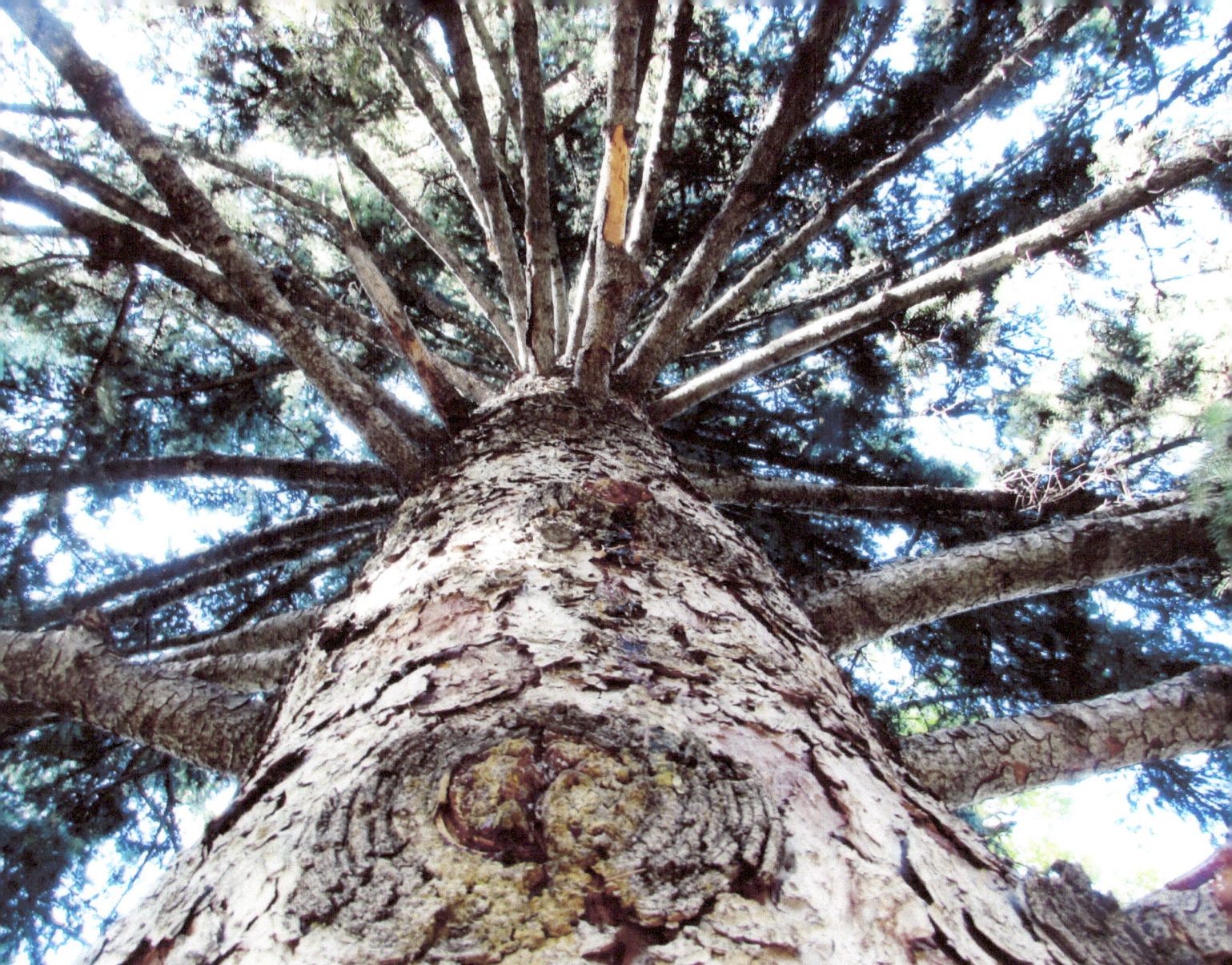

Would You Rather?

Would you love me if I split my ribs?
If I opened my belly and let my innards fall,
baring what was within me for your judgment,
Would you be struck with terror?

Or would you rather I hide it all under
This thin veil of skin I wear when under the sun?

Would you look wistfully in my eyes
if I cracked my skull and dug deeply
into grey matter to pull out and display my secret
thoughts about the Universe?

Or would you rather I put them in a poem
that seeks to find all that is beautiful as it is?

Would you hold me closely if I tore my bones out
and lining them end to end so you could see what
keeps me upright, straight and tall
under clouds and sunshine alike?

Or would you rather hold me close, squeezing
to feel them beneath my layers?

Would you long for me if I peeled away my skin,
stretching it out to leather under hot suns
to show you how truly thin the membrane
containing my spirit is?

Or would should I gently touch you, passing volts
between us – flesh to flesh?

Would you weep with me in joy if I split my veins
spilling every drop of my blood
to form a gushing river of my passions
uncontained?

Or would you rather I look deeply into your eyes
and smile into your soul?

19

The Transient

It is Friday, again. This living street is thriving and volatile. Oblivious to the world around and within it, it has become feral. Danny, however, is not oblivious to the world within him. He is quite aware of the world around him as well, even if he is unable to wear evidence in his expression. But he desires oblivion, that he could simply flip some switch and turn it all off and force darkness and silence on both worlds. He sees it all. The city lights blink with activity, disappearing in the shadows of people walking by and then reappearing, some sort of dull orange on the un-white, un-grey cement of the sidewalk. He watches as people nearly trip over him, but makes no move to protect himself because he knows they will not bring themselves to touch him. He huddles against the brick wall hugging his knees as if they are an inconsolable child demanding an impossible consolation. The space in front of the toes of his shoes form a rounded lowercase m. m is for memory m is for memory, he does not bother an attempt to turn off the running mantra that gushes through his conscious mind; in fact, the mantra sometimes veils the memory it beckons. A part of him wonders – the part, he supposes, that once was sane – if he has somehow become partly invisible: he can be seen, but only in the same way one notices a mud puddle, something to avoid. He cares about that part least of all though; it has never really served him well.

Tonight is the night; he just feels it whispered in the air as a secret from a lover. He wants the embrace of death to bring an end to the constant, obsessive torrent of recollections his mind forces him to replay. He desires that embrace in the same way he once desired her embrace – it is the type of embrace that transcends physical love; it is the type that has created a vocabulary shared only by two; it is the type that brings definition to who you are. But until he receives that embrace, he suffers the constant flow of that torrential memory.

That day was a Friday too:

He was able to get off work early, and was excited to begin the weekend sooner than they had planned. He and Beth – she was so beautiful – were going to spend the weekend at a cabin up north he had reserved and paid for months ago. He was supposed to be off at six o'clock, but at noon, his manager handed him his paycheck, patted him on the shoulder and apologized. No need to say you're sorry, Danny thought, it's dead and there's no need for two waiters. He absently folded the envelope in half and stuffed it in his back pocket. Though he needed every penny he could get, surely he could sacrifice a couple hours in order to take his soon-to-be, hopefully, fiancé to the cabin early.

I can ask her tonight, his thought provoked reverie: he would ask her on the lake at sunset; they would row out to the middle, the part where the reflection of the trees surrounded them and remained uninterrupted as if they were floating listlessly on a cloud gazing out at parallel universes both filled with lush forests holding up a sky that joined at the exact spot their boat rested upon. It would be perfect.

His MP3 player blasting through the earbuds and the distraction of his awesome mood were the causes of his failure to notice the rhythmic noise emanating from the bedroom as he examined the unopened mail on the console table – all of it was for Beth – and quietly shut the door behind him.

"Bethy, baby," he yelled. The thought floated somewhere in his dreamy state that she should be parked on the couch watching her soap, but the TV screen was black and the couch was empty and looked cold. How odd? Maybe she's taking a nap, he thought, and pointed his half-dancing feet toward the hallway.

As he walked down the narrow passageway, he remembered when he moved in and tried to fit his king-sized box-spring through the bedroom door: There was no way. They could only manage to get it wedged between the door jamb and the opposite wall of the hallway. It was Beth's idea to just get rid of it and set the mattress on the floor, "It'll be an adventure," she argued, "Plus, you won't fall out of bed when you're sick." He pushed the oversized boxspring against the hallway wall and growled, "It happened one time!" She ran screaming and giggling down the hall and tried to slide the bedroom door shut before he could get to her, shrieking with laughter. She did not fight very hard though when he caught her. She definitely did not fight as he traced her jaw from chin to ear with the back of his finger and down her neck and then to her breast, where he turned his finger over and traced the outline of her protruding nipple through her thin tee and proceeded to press his lips to hers. She did not fight as they made love.

A movement in his peripheral snagged his attention from his reverie. He looked up to see Beth standing in the doorway of their bedroom holding a sheet to her chest, and apparently nothing else. She was sweaty and her hidden nudity fought with his concern that she might be sick. In his current reverie, he thought that perhaps the trip could be delayed for a bit more, but the look of terror on her face brought his hackles up.

"Wait," he said as he began to piece together what was happening. The sheet, the look of terror, the smell of rose incense – her favorite aphrodisiac – the fact that she would have no idea he would be home early, all these led to the realization that she might not be alone and just as if on cue, a man poked his head from behind the door, followed by the rest of him, wearing nothing but a pillow. The realization dropped from Danny's throat like a hydrogen bomb and landed at the bottom of his gut with enough force that he physically shuddered.

"Danny, I…" the man said.

The pillow-wearing-son-of-a-bitch was his best friend John. He had introduced Beth and Danny.

"What the fuck?"

The events that occurred next were a blur, disjointed scenes with fuzz-colored ideas and words spoken by him and them and her all at the same time with yelling and crying and begging and bare flesh exposed accidentally when arms waving in accusation and justification forgot they held a sheet to cover bare breasts. Danny paused, wide-mouthed when the sheet fell. Her breasts, those perfect beautiful breasts, were covered in sweat and the filth of betrayal.

To this point in the chaos, there had been no violence, but Danny tuned out the cacophony and stared at those breasts for what seemed like an eternity and all he could see, and he realized that all he would ever see was another man's hands all over them, so he reacted without thinking and struck a breast with his fingertips.

Beth fell to the floor, clutching her offended bosom and John reacted by throwing a wild punch that landed squarely on Danny's forehead who was knocked unconscious almost immediately. When he awoke, he was on the couch; Beth was fully clothed, and holding an ice pack against the side of her left breast, where he had hit her.

She extended the ice pack and, with a pouty expression that looked like sympathy and apology, motioned it toward his head. He reached up to feel and discovered a large bump.

"John left," Beth said, "He said it was too much for him and didn't want to get involved… that fucking asshole."

STOP! Danny thought, no, screamed at the obsessive voice attempting to become the sole occupant his mind. NO MORE! He could no longer bear the flood of recollection that replayed over and over and over of that night. Tonight, finally, would be the night he would find that peace he so desperately craved. Perhaps the idea of peace was aiming too high; he just did not want to hurt anymore. He did not want to feel… anything.

Besides, it wasn't just her, it was everything. It took only a matter of a couple days for Danny's life to come crashing down around him, to a pile of rubble strewn beyond the borders of epic failure. He lost the woman he loved, his best friend, his job, his home… everything he could claim to be his.

He had decided to go to the cabin anyway, and had no problem asking Beth for the use of her car, which, likely out of guilt, she agreed. It was a simple plan and easily formed: be alone, drink, pass out… forget. The last, he would never do.

When he arrived at the cabin, evening had fallen and the moon replaced the sun and brought with it a chill that begged for a sweater. The song of the woods and the gentle lapping of the lake filled the air with calm and peace and hope for rejuvenation. The soft, meditative sounds and the piney forest aromas wafted along calming currents of air reached out and invited Danny to stroll, and commune and cry and heal. Screw that, he thought, I'm getting shitfaced. He did not bother unpacking; I probably won't even change my clothes over the weekend. So he tossed his small suitcase somewhere on the floor, next to the glass-topped coffee table framed with polished cedar, like all the furniture in this of this two story, loft-cabin. When he opened the door he was blasted with the odor of cedar and pine, an odor that reminded him of freshly cut Christmas trees brought in from the cold and thawed by the warmth of a fireplace – his last Christmas memory from childhood when he was six. The couch in the center of the room was a well-crafted futon, disguised by its rustic design to appear like an old wooden bench with new padding. That was where spent the entire weekend; he did not bother turning it into a bed.

He plopped down on the over-soft mattress and the crinkle in his back pocket reminded him that he had forgotten to deposit his paycheck. No big deal, he told himself, I'll drop it off on my way to work on Monday. He leaned against the back of the futon straightening his body and reached to pull the folded envelope from his back pocket and proceeded to tear the side off in order to extract the contents which consisted of his check, which was as much as he expected it to be, and something else, in the form of a folded piece of paper which revealed a document on the company letterhead with his name hand written on a printed blank line at the top and some phrases that immediately jumped out: deeply regret to inform you; due to the economy; decided to downsize; unfortunately, you were not considered to be invaluable.

I guess no one considers me to be invaluable, and then he began to drink.

That weekend went by faster than he preferred. Sunday woke him at noon with blurred memories of the previous couple days and possibly the worst headache, driest mouth and guck-filled eyes of his life. After a gulp of water, he realized that the musky stench he smelled was himself and decided bathing would be appropriate.

The warm water washed over his face forming streams that poured from his nose and chin that joined together and landed on the floor of the ceramic basin with a tinny clang that was much too loud. Though his head throbbed, he stayed in the shower until the warmth began to run out, and soon regretted the speed he was forced to scrape soap over his body, rip shampoo through his hair and then rinse in water that was far too cold to help ease the thudding in his head.

After drying off, Danny wiped a circle in the steam covered mirror to reveal a slightly distorted version of the face he had come to know over the course of his life, a face he now hated. His disgust formed in a pain filled scowl hidden behind broken lines of globulous water drops that clung to the mirror in swirl-like patterns. He felt adrenaline seep into his empty spaces. His veins stretched and spilled over to fill his face with a flush of rage. His heated face began to tighten with the pressure and drew the scowl deeper until it took control and struck. Tears and rage washed over his face, distorting the already blurred vision looking back at him and he wondered if it was he or his reflection that had become so distorted. He struck again with all his strength.

The crashing shatter twinkled in a chorus of surprise – or was it mockery? His reflection disappeared and now he had a new problem, a mangled hand. The studious and painful extraction of glass from knuckles and fingers had a few unexpected effects: it calmed him down, he became completely oblivious to his headache and though he had not consciously realized it had become an option, it convinced him that he did not have courage enough to slice open his wrists. He also had not consciously realized that he wanted to die, until now and so he began to plan.

No memories exist of the drive home, only knowledge that he had not attempted veering off the edge of a high mountain road. He did remember, as he unlocked the door to the apartment he called home for two years, the depth of his desire to see her sitting on the couch, amid a bank of used tissues, waiting for him – waiting to say she was sorry, that she had made a horrible mistake and really realized that she only wanted to love him like she knew he loved her and if he could only just forgive her she would spend the rest of her life regaining his trust and… But the apartment was empty.

The entry way greeted him with a stack of cardboard boxes topped with a piece of paper neatly folded and prominently displayed. He took it to the empty couch and read:

Daniel,

I packed all of your stuff into these three boxes. I am spending the night at my sister's house and will be back tomorrow after I get off work at 5:00. I know you have nowhere to go, so please stay here tonite and double check to make sure I didn't miss any of your belongings. I know the mattress is yours and if you want it down the road, I'll not fight you for it.

I want you to know that, I'm so very sorry for my part in all this. I handled it badly. I should have come to you sooner. I had planned to tell you over the weekend, but… well, I guess, the best laid plans of mice and men, huh? I hope you take care of yourself.

Beth

p.s. John freaked out and took off. I talked to his landlord yesterday & she said that he paid up to the end of the month, gave notice and told her to keep the deposit. He didn't tell anyone where he was going. Fucking asshole!!!

He crumpled the note and wept. He had no more energy for rage. He could feel himself slipping into an abysmal depression. One more night in this apartment. It was too quiet. He couldn't wait any longer. He didn't wait. It was time to initiate his plan.

The medicine cabinet held the same reflection as the mirror in the cabin had, but this time, it was a clear image staring back at him and no longer angry; it was pathetic, sad, no… it was worthless. He didn't rush to open the door, but he also did not linger on the face looking back at him which now seemed so ugly and unlovable to him. No wonder she left you, you stupid piece of shit, he thought, regaining a flash of anger that lasted only a moment as the swinging door hid the putrid face and revealed a plethora of brown bottles and white lids and faintly visible outlines of pills and… release.

Some hours later, Danny was huddled up over the toilet seat heaving up what could only be his guts: what was in them had been expelled long ago. He was sick. Very sick. But not dead.

Time began to slip away beyond the need for definition as he felt himself slipping in and out of consciousness. Those moments of consciousness were surprisingly lucid. The moments in between were strangely more lucid. He came to, and the world spun in high definition: a urine stain on the back of the toilet seat lid that had the same basic shape as the state of Florida, the odor of it stung the back of his tongue, a chip in the tub that stood out black against the stark whiteness of the porcelain, the dull green diamonds in ivory squares of linoleum were interrupted by the shag U-shaped carpet that surrounded the base of the toilet, and a faint line unhidden under paint between sheets of drywall he had never noticed before.

But those other moments, the ones between bouts of wakefulness were something else entirely. Is this what they mean, he thought he was only thinking it, but could clearly hear his own voice, which had the dreamy quality of a lullaby resting in the ears of a small, frightened child now too sleepy to remain awake, when they say your life flashes before your eyes? Visions of his life flew past from memories he had not realized he retained. He saw a moment from his sixth birthday party when he looked up into his mother's face and saw an expression that exuded love and pride and felt it fulfilling him. It was just a moment, but a moment in his life when he knew that he was loved. He saw a moment from his first date with Beth when he had told a joke – a stupid joke – but she laughed anyway – a nervous laugh – which set him at ease but only just a little; she was so beautiful and so far out of his league, but he was comforted knowing she was nervous too. They both wanted this date to go well and this, he knew in his reverie, was the seed of love that might grow between them.

Then he would drift back into the bathroom which seemed as if it just might become his tomb – not light-bright enough for a bathroom and too small. The idea grew into a regret that was blanketed by his newfound clarity. I don't really wanna die, he just did not want to hurt this much.

And then he was back in some distant, vague memory that began to shed that vagueness like one does a raincoat when going inside. And then as suddenly, he was back in the bathroom. Clarity was gone. He was eddying in and out of reality. This time, he heard strange voices and saw strange faces – either real or imagined, he could not tell, but not remembered – imposing upon his vision and he wondered how these people came to fit in this tiny pastel cartoon bathroom.

The process of switching back and forth became so confusing that he was no longer sure if he was conscious: he could blink and be in a different world. He floated on his back down the hallway and through the living room and then he floated on his back in his neighbors swimming pool when he was twelve and was just not ready to get out of the water. He heard Beth's voice frantically relaying some story of finding someone on her bathroom floor and then he remembered getting far too drunk at a friend's party in high school and ended up passing out on their bathroom floor with his hand stuck in the toilet. He recognized the interior of the elevator of his apartment complex and a stain on the ceiling that he first saw when Beth had first brought him here. Now there was a man and a woman dressed in white hovering on each side of him and something was on his face. The woman was talking to him, "Hang in there Daniel, we're gonna take good care of you. Just hang in there."

He tried to respond, "I don't know who you are. I don't remember you," but whatever it was on his face made it too difficult to speak. On some odd level, he found it humorous, but instead of laughing, he smiled and all went black.

Beth sat across the hall from Danny's hospital door. She was not crying anymore; she had been all cried out. She felt guilty, yes, but more numb than anything else. They had pumped his stomach and she was grateful when they told her that he had vomited most of the pills, which was probably what saved his life.

"Does he have any family in the area," a nurse had asked.

"He doesn't have any family anywhere," Beth replied, "He never had any siblings and both his parents died when he was seven." This was the worst part of it all. She and John were all that Danny really had. This was probably why he did what he did; he didn't have anywhere to go or anyone to turn to. Nothing about him stood out to anyone. He was average in just about everything he did, which was probably why she had done what she had done. She knew that he loved her, probably more deeply than anyone else ever would, definitely more deeply than she deserved. But their life together had grown stagnant and she was bored. She didn't think about how it would affect him. She was young. She wanted to just be young. She suspected he was thinking about marriage, but she couldn't bring herself to consider it as an option, not yet. She wanted to live a little before she settled down and Danny was just not the kind of guy you dated when you wanted to have fun. If they would have only met a few years later, things might have been different.

She would be ok, though. She had family and friends and plenty of support. As for Danny, he had none. She didn't know what to do. So, she did the only thing she could, and left.

But none of that is important. It is Friday again, and Danny sits against a brick building thinking once again about Beth. He really doesn't know how long it has been, but her face is now fuzzy in his memory. It could have been three of four weeks ago, maybe more than a year, maybe even more than that. His hair is now gray– is that a clue? It doesn't matter. What matters was that it is Friday and soon, he would know the warm embrace of a new lover. Soon, he would have the courage to meet her and dance with her and love her. And she would love him too. And he would no longer be alone.

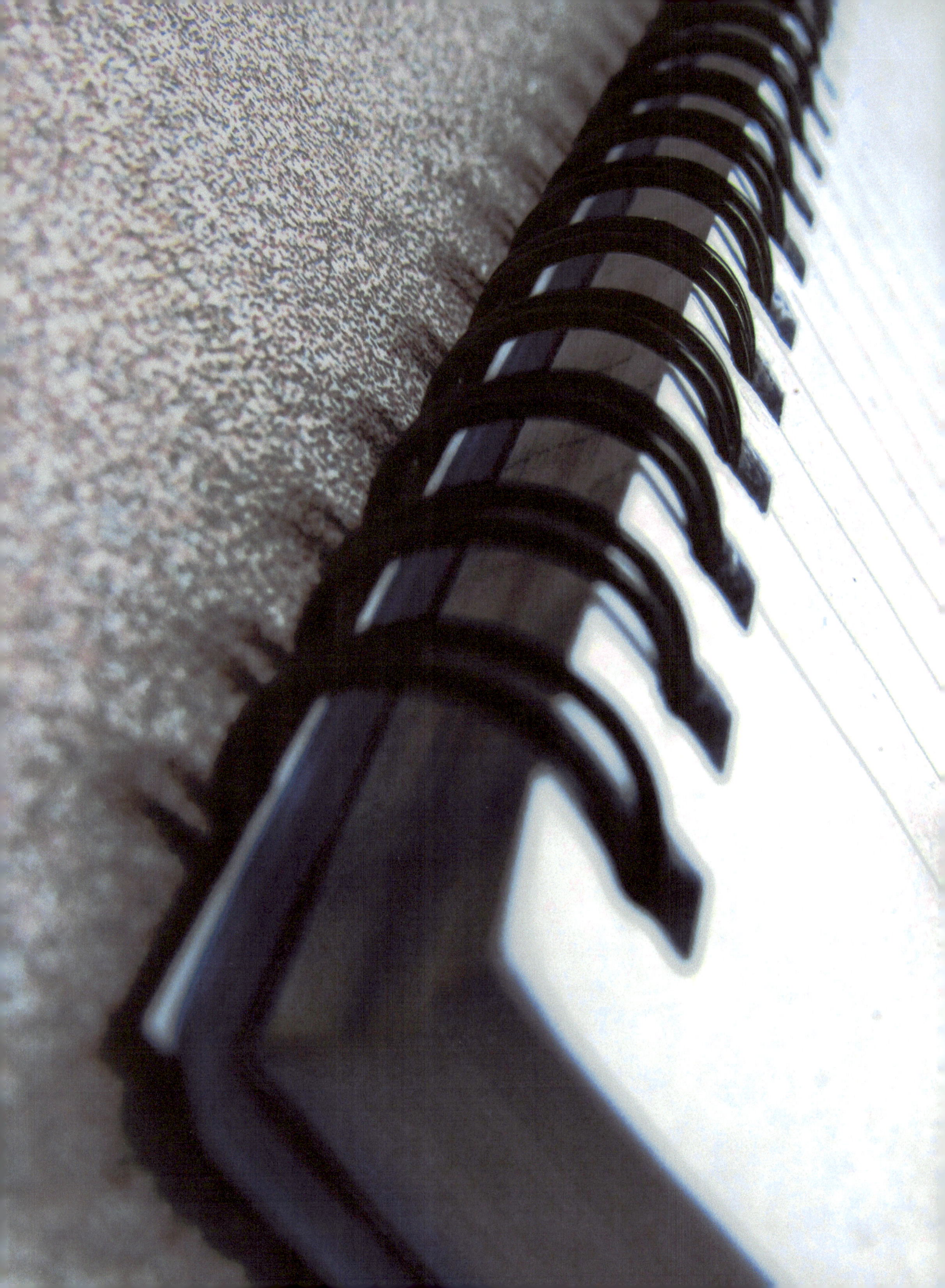